WISCONSIN
TRAVEL GUIDE
2023-2024

Discover the Charm of America's Dairyland

FRANK T. LESTER

WISCONSIN TRAVEL GUIDE 2023-2024

Discover the Charm of America's Dairyland

Frank T. Lester

Table of contents

Introduction   7
Chapter 1: Planning Your Trip   **10**
   Creating Your Itinerary   10
   Ideal Season to Visit   12
   Planning a Budget for a Wisconsin Adventure   13
Chapter 2: Getting to Wisconsin   **16**
   Transportation Options   16
   Airports in Wisconsin   18
   Navigating the Roadways   19
Chapter 3: Examining the Regions of Wisconsin   **22**
   Southern Wisconsin   22
      Milwaukee: Brew City Delights   23
      Madison: The Capital Experience 24
      Green County: Swiss Heritage   26
   Central Wisconsin   28
      Wisconsin Dells: Waterpark Capital of the World 28
      Wausau: Centre for Outdoor Recreation 30
      Stevens Point: Culture and the Arts 31
   Northern Wisconsin   33
      Hayward: Freshwater Fishing Paradise 34
      Bayfield: Apostle Islands Adventure 35
      Rhinelander: A Beauty of the North 37
Chapter 4: Accommodations   **39**
   Resorts and Hotels   39
   Cozy Cottages and Cabins   43

RV parks and campgrounds   44

Unique Accommodations: Treehouses and Lighthouses   45

Chapter 5: Dining and Culinary Delights   **48**

Wisconsin's Culinary Traditions   48

Cheese Trails and Dairy Destinations   50

Farm-to-Table Dining   51

Wineries and Craft Breweries   52

Chapter 6: Outdoor Adventures   **54**

Biking Trails and Hiking   54

Water Sports: Kayaking, Canoeing, and Fishing   56

Winter Sports: Skiing and Snowmobiling   57

Chapter 7: Family-Friendly Fun   **60**

Waterparks and Amusement Parks   60

Animal Encounters at Zoos   62

Science Centres and Children's Museums   63

Chapter 8: Culture and The Arts   **64**

Historical and Museum Locations   65

Performing Arts and Art Galleries   67

Chapter 9: Festivals & Events   **69**

The Year-Round Festivals in Wisconsin   69

Important Dates Calendar   71

Chapter 10: Practical Information   **74**

Safety Advice for Travel   74

Packing Advice   76

Maps and Navigation   77

Chapter 11: Hidden Gems and Local Tips   **80**

Off-the-Beaten-Track Excursions   80

Local Favourites   82

Chapter 12: Beyond Wisconsin   **86**

    Day Trips to Neighboring States   86

    Combining the Great Lakes   88

Conclusion   **92**

Appendix   **96**

    Useful Resources   96

        Contact details   98

        Tourist Information Centers   98

Index   **101**

    Detailed Index for Quick Reference   101

Bonus: Travel Journal   **109**

Introduction

Welcome to Wisconsin, a state known for its stunning natural scenery, diverse population, and gracious people. Wisconsin, a state famous for making cheese and having rolling farmlands, is located in the middle of America's Midwest and is frequently referred to as "America's Dairyland." But Wisconsin's offerings go far beyond its history as a dairy state. It is a state bursting with interesting sights and sounds, from energetic metropolises to tranquil rural settings.

This travel guide will help you discover the secrets of Wisconsin as you set out on your tour through this lovely state. Whether you're an adventure enthusiast, a history buff, a foodie, or a family seeking an unforgettable vacation, our guide is designed to meet your needs.

The chapters that follow will take you on a thorough tour of Wisconsin's many regions. You'll go through Milwaukee's busy streets, where breweries and museums live peacefully. Discover the vibrant, culturally diverse capital of Madison and lose yourself in the breathtaking natural beauty of Green County, which has Swiss roots.

Wisconsin won't let down adventurers looking for outdoor activities. Your inner explorer will be satisfied as you discover comprehensive information on hiking routes, water activities, winter sports, and hidden jewels in every location. And don't forget to check out our suggestions for family-friendly amusement parks, zoos, and kid-friendly museums where fun and education may coexist.

The food scene in Wisconsin is quite delightful. Eat at farm-to-table establishments, sample award-winning cheeses, and enjoy specialty beverages. Our guide offers details on the state's culinary customs and must-see attractions.

This travel guide wants to be your go-to resource whether you're organizing a solo trip, a family holiday, or a romantic break. We've got you covered with useful advice as well as local favorites and undiscovered discoveries.

Prepare to fall in love with Wisconsin's charm, variety of scenery, and friendly people as you read through the pages of this guide. Wisconsin is an experience rather than just a place to visit. Therefore, let's embark on this amazing tour, uncovering Wisconsin's riches and making lifelong memories.

Chapter 1: Planning Your Trip

Making a well-considered itinerary is crucial before setting out on a vacation to discover Wisconsin's wonder and beauty. It is essential to tailor your trip to your interests and tastes because Wisconsin has a vast variety of activities and sights. We will walk you through the process of creating a well-structured itinerary in this part.

Creating Your Itinerary

1. Establish the Duration: Decide how long you'll be in Wisconsin in the beginning. The length of your stay will affect the locations and activities you can take part in, whether it's a quick weekend escape or a lengthy vacation.

2. Determine Your Interests: Wisconsin has a wide variety of experiences to choose from. Are you interested in water activities and hiking paths outside? Or maybe you're more interested in cultural events and delectable cuisine. To help you plan your trip, consider your interests.

3. Pick Your Regions: Wisconsin is segregated into various areas, each of which has its distinctive charms. Will you visit the busy metropolis of Milwaukee and Madison or would you rather enjoy the peace of the lakes and forests in northern Wisconsin? Choose the areas that correspond to your interests.

4. Sort Must-See Attractions by Priority: Do some research on the must-see sights in the areas you intend to visit. List the things that are at the top of your itinerary, whether they are the historical sites in Prairie du Chien, the waterparks in Wisconsin Dells, or the art galleries in Milwaukee.

5. Schedule Your Daily Activities: Describe your schedule day by day. Choose the sights you'll go to, the restaurants you'll eat at, and the activities you'll do. To make sure your strategy can be executed, take into account the closing times of museums, parks, and other locations.

Ideal Season to Visit

Wisconsin has four distinct seasons, so when you visit can have a big impact on how you feel. Making the most of your vacation will depend on your knowledge about the ideal time to travel:

• **Summer (June to August):** This is the busiest travel time of the year because of the warm, pleasant weather that is perfect for outdoor activities. Water activities, hiking, and discovering Wisconsin's festivals are all ideal in the summer.

• **Autumn (September to November):** As the leaves change color, autumn in Wisconsin offers breathtaking scenery. It's a great time to go trekking, take scenic drives, and go to autumn festivals.

• **Winter (December to February):** This is the time of year to enjoy winter sports like skiing and snowmobiling. It's a wonderful opportunity to engage in cozy inside activities as Wisconsin changes into a winter paradise.

- **Spring (March to May):** Spring is a great season to go trekking and explore gardens because the weather is milder. The tourism season is also less busy.

Planning a Budget for a Wisconsin Adventure

Planning a trip requires careful consideration of your money. Different budgets can find possibilities in Wisconsin, but it's important to know your budgetary constraints:

- **Accommodations:** Do your research and reserve your lodging much in advance. Budget-friendly motels, opulent resorts, and inviting cottages are all possibilities. Depending on the time of year and the location, the rates can differ greatly.

- **Transportation:** Take into account both your means of entry and exit from Wisconsin. There are practical alternatives including taxis, trains, and even rental cars.

- **Activities:** Budget for the price of any entertainment, meals, and entrance fees to attractions. When traveling with a family, especially, keep an eye out for discounts and special deals.

- **Miscellaneous Expenses:** Be sure to include money in your budget for extras like souvenirs, petrol, and unforeseen costs. Having a safety net in your budget for unforeseen expenses is always a good idea.

You can ensure that your vacation to Wisconsin is not only fun but also well-organized, making the most of your stay in this interesting state, by carefully planning your schedule, picking the perfect time to visit, and budgeting sensibly.

Chapter 2: Getting to Wisconsin

It's important to think about your transportation options as you get ready to travel to Wisconsin to enjoy its delights. The mode of transportation you select can have a big impact on how you feel about your trip to Wisconsin because the state has a variety of landscapes. We'll look at the many modes of transit in this section to help you get to and around Wisconsin.

Transportation Options

1. By Car: Driving is a great alternative for those who want flexibility and the chance to explore Wisconsin's hidden corners. You can travel picturesque routes and reach more isolated regions by bringing your vehicle or renting one. The well-maintained road system in Wisconsin makes road excursions a common choice.

2. By Air: Flying into Wisconsin is a practical option if you're coming from a distance or want to save time. The main entry points into Wisconsin are Green Bay Austin Straubel International Airport, Madison Dane County Regional Airport, and Milwaukee Mitchell International Airport. These airports make flying accessible by providing a variety of domestic and international flights.

3. By Train: Wisconsin is accessible by Amtrak's Empire Builder and Hiawatha lines. The Empire Builder Line travels through Wisconsin and connects places including Milwaukee, Wisconsin Dells, La Crosse, and more, while the Hiawatha Line extends from Milwaukee to Chicago. A distinctive and beautiful way to get to Wisconsin is by train.

4. By Bus: Wisconsin is serviced by several bus companies, making this a cheap mode of transportation. Connecting major cities including Milwaukee, Madison, and Green Bay are the Greyhound and Megabus routes. It's a cost-effective choice for vacationers.

5. By Bike: Wisconsin provides fantastic biking opportunities for the daring and environmentally-minded traveler. You can explore the state's picturesque landscapes at your own pace thanks to the state's bike-friendly infrastructure, which includes paths and lanes.

Airports in Wisconsin

1. Milwaukee Mitchell International Airport (MKE): Situated only a few miles from Milwaukee's city center, MKE is Wisconsin's biggest and busiest airport. It serves as a handy entry point for travelers with its extensive selection of domestic and international flights.

2. Madison Dane County Regional Airport (MSN): MSN is a medium-sized airport that serves Madison, the state's capital, and has links to important American cities. Visitors to the city frequently choose it because of its proximity to Madison.

3. Green Bay Austin Straubel International Airport (GRB): This airport, which is located in

Green Bay, offers connections to numerous locations, mostly within the United States. Travelers interested in exploring northeastern Wisconsin should consider it.

Navigating the Roadways

Whether you arrive in Wisconsin by plane, train, or bus, you'll probably need to use the state's roads to get where you're going or check out its attractions. The following are some navigational advice:

- **Road Quality:** In general, Wisconsin's roads are well-kept and simple to use. Interstates 94, 90, and 43 connect important cities and areas.

- **Rental Cars:** If you forgot to bring your vehicle, renting one is a practical choice. At airports and in cities all around the state, there are a lot of rental companies.

- **Public Transit:** You can rely on public transit, such as buses and trams, for city travel in urban regions like Milwaukee and Madison.

- **Scenic Drives:** Wisconsin has several beautiful backroads. For a fascinating adventure, think about using the Great River Road or the Lake Superior Scenic Byway.

- **Traffic Conditions:** Keep an eye out for traffic, especially during busy travel times or during significant events. To avoid traffic, make appropriate travel time plans.

Wisconsin offers a range of transport alternatives to fit your requirements and interests, whether you prefer the independence of a road trip, the effectiveness of air travel, or the charm of train or bus excursions. Your journey to and within the state will be smoother and more pleasurable if you are aware of these options.

Chapter 3: Examining the Regions of Wisconsin

Southern Wisconsin

Southern Wisconsin is an area with a diverse population and stunning natural surroundings that combines metropolitan energy with small-town charm. We'll take you on a tour of Southern Wisconsin in this part of our travel guide, emphasizing the distinctive experiences you can look forward to in its vivacious cities and peaceful countryside.

Milwaukee: Brew City Delights

Wisconsin's largest metropolis and "Brew City," Milwaukee, is a mecca for cultural and gastronomic adventures. Here are some things you can anticipate in this vibrant city:

1. Brewery Tours: are popular in Milwaukee, which is known for its brewery culture. Experience guided tours and tastings at renowned breweries including MillerCoors, Lakefront Brewery, and Pabst Brewery.

2. Lakefront Activities: Milwaukee, which is located on the western shore of Lake Michigan, offers lovely lakefront strolls, bike rides, and water sports. Visit the Milwaukee Art Museum, which is famous for its spectacular architecture.

3. Food Scene: Choose from a variety of dining establishments, including gourmet dining and traditional German beer halls. Cheese curds, a local delicacy, should not be missed.

4. Ancient Neighbourhoods: Stroll through ancient areas like the Third Ward to uncover distinctive shops, art galleries, and mouthwatering food markets.

Madison: The Capital Experience

The state capital of Wisconsin, Madison, is an intriguing visit due to its combination of political clout and scenic beauty:

1. State Capitol Building: Tour the magnificent Wisconsin State Capitol, a work of architecture. Learn about its history on a guided tour, then ascend to the observation deck for sweeping vistas.

2. University of Wisconsin-Madison: Explore the active campus of the University of Wisconsin-Madison, which is home to lovely gardens, museums, and cultural events.

3. Outdoor Activities: Madison is surrounded by parks and lakes, providing possibilities for picnics, hiking, and kayaking. Visit the Olbrich Botanical Gardens as soon as possible.

4. Farmers' Markets: Visit the largest in the nation, the Dane County Farmers' Market. Enjoy live music, handcrafted items, and fresh veggies.

Green County: Swiss Heritage

Green County, located in southern Wisconsin, is renowned for its Swiss ancestry, gently undulating terrain, and quaint tiny towns:

1. Swiss Cheese and Chocolate: Explore the Swiss influence by savoring local cheese and indulging in Swiss chocolates in New Glarus, which is sometimes referred to as "America's Little Switzerland."

2. Historical Sites: In New Glarus, the Swiss Historical Village allows you to travel back in time and discover more about the early residents of the area.

3. Countryside Drives: Green County has beautiful scenery and winding roads. The tranquil setting for unhurried exploring is provided by the undulating hills and dairy farms.

4. Monroe: Visit the charming town square in the county seat of Monroe. Dine on Swiss food in nearby restaurants and visit the National Historic Cheesemaking Centre.

The combination of urban energy and rural beauty in southern Wisconsin offers a variety of experiences for all kinds of tourists. This area offers something unique in store for everyone, whether you're drawn to the cultural wonders of Milwaukee, the political drama of Madison, or the Swiss legacy of Green County.

Central Wisconsin

With its natural beauty and variety of activities, Central Wisconsin is a location that appeals to outdoor enthusiasts, families, and cultural vultures alike. This section of our travel guide will take you on a tour of Central Wisconsin while showcasing the distinctive experiences that await you there.

Wisconsin Dells: Waterpark Capital of the World

The "Waterpark Capital of the World" moniker belongs to Wisconsin Dells for good reason. It's a place with never-ending excitement and fun:

1. Waterpacks Galore: There are a tonne of waterparks in Wisconsin Dells, both indoor and outdoor, to keep guests of all ages entertained. There is something for everyone, from exhilarating slides to relaxing rivers.

2. Scenic Dells: Take a boat excursion down the Wisconsin River to discover the breathtaking natural beauty of the Dells. It's breathtaking to see the distinctive sandstone cliffs, canyons, and rock formations.

3. Outdoor Activities: In addition to waterparks, the region also has picturesque trails, ziplining, and hiking. Additionally, there are several opportunities for golfing, boating, and fishing.

4. Entertainment and Dining: Take advantage of the exciting nightlife that includes live performances, magic shows, and a variety of exotic and traditional American cuisines.

Wausau: Centre for Outdoor Recreation

Wausau is a haven for outdoor enthusiasts, offering a variety of activities situated amidst beautiful scenery:

1. Rib Mountain State Park: Explore the park's hiking, biking, and skiing paths. It becomes a sanctuary for skiing and snowboarding in the winter.

2. Granite Peak: Discover Granite Peak, the top ski resort in the Midwest, with its varied terrain and slopes for skiers of all levels.

3. Kayaking and canoeing: Try your hand at these water sports on the Wisconsin River or one of the numerous surrounding lakes.

4. Arts & Culture: Check out the Yawkey House Museum or the Leigh Yawkey Woodson Art Museum, both of which are noted for their distinctive works of art with bird themes.

Stevens Point: Culture and the Arts

The town of Stevens Point combines creative expression with cultural encounters:

1. University of Wisconsin-Steven Point: The theatre, music, and arts programs of the University of Wisconsin-Stevens Point provide a thriving cultural scene. All year round, go to concerts and exhibits.

2. Museums: Visit the Museum of Natural History, which is renowned for its dinosaur exhibitions, and the Stevens Point Sculpture Park, which features outdoor artwork.

3. Local Breweries: Breweries like Central Waters Brewing Company, where you can sample artisan beers and take brewery tours, are located in Stevens Point.

4. Green Circle Trail: Explore the city on foot or by bicycle along the 27-mile Green Circle Trail, which offers stunning views of the surrounding countryside.

A rich cultural tapestry, calm natural settings, and fun waterparks are all perfectly combined in Central Wisconsin. Central Wisconsin has something for everyone, whether you want to have fun in the waterparks of Wisconsin Dells, discover the great outdoors in Wausau, or immerse yourself in the arts and culture of Stevens Point.

Northern Wisconsin

In Northern Wisconsin, there are several unspoiled lakes, lush woods, and outdoor recreation opportunities. Explore Northern Wisconsin in this part of our travel guide, where the great outdoors takes center stage.

Hayward: Freshwater Fishing Paradise

With so many lakes and rivers for freshwater fishing, Hayward is a sanctuary for fishermen and outdoor enthusiasts:

1. Fishing Possibilities: Muskellunge, walleye, bass, and panfish are among the world-class fish that may be caught in Hayward. Some of the best places to fish include Nelson Lake and the Chippewa Flowage.

2. Explore the National Fresh Water Fishing Hall of Fame to learn about the tradition and skill of freshwater fishing and to see the famous huge muskie statue.

3. Outdoor Activities: In addition to fishing, the Chequamegon-Nicolet National Forest near Hayward provides possibilities for hiking, boating, and animal viewing.

4. Lumberjack Shows: With engaging lumberjack shows, you may take in the thrill of lumberjack competitions and discover the area's wood heritage.

Bayfield: Apostle Islands Adventure

The enchanting Apostle Islands are accessible from Bayfield, which is situated on the beaches of Lake Superior, offering several chances for exploration:

1. Apostle Islands Cruises: Take a boat cruise to see the magnificent lighthouses, sea caves, and Lake Superior's natural splendor. The islands provide unmatched opportunities for sailing and kayaking.

2. Outdoor activities: Go camping, hike the paths on Madeline Island or the mainland, or take pictures of wildlife and birds at the Apostle Islands National Lakeshore.

3. Fruit Orchards: Bayfield is well-known for its apple orchards. Visit in the autumn to indulge in fresh apples and take part in harvest celebrations.

4. Arts & Culture: Discover the lively culture of the area in Bayfield's theatres, music festivals, and art galleries.

Rhinelander: A Beauty of the North

The epitome of a Northwoods getaway, Rhinelander is where the outdoors reigns supreme:

1. Outdoor Paradise: Soak up the lovely Northwoods atmosphere. Enjoy the state parks and woods nearby for hiking, camping, and snowmobiling.

2. Boating and Watersports: Fishing, boating, and water activities are all quite popular in the area because of the many clear lakes that dot the landscape.

3. Wildlife Sightings: Rhinelander is situated in "Hodag Country," which is renowned for the legendary Hodag beast. Learn about this local myth and visit natural preserves to see the region's rich animals.

4. History and heritage: Go to the Logging Museum, which provides information on the lengthy history of the logging business in the Northwoods. Visit the Northwoods Children's Museum for a fun experience with the whole family.

Northern Wisconsin offers an immersive experience in the heart of nature with its world-class fishing, island excursions, and Northwoods splendor. This area provides an outdoor paradise for everyone who seeks it, whether you're fishing for the "big catch" in Hayward, discovering the beauty of the Apostle Islands in Bayfield, or soaking in the peace of the Northwoods in Rhinelander.

Chapter 4: Accommodations

There is a wide variety of lodging options to select from while making travel plans to Wisconsin. The state's hotels and resorts provide a broad range of choices, each catering to various tastes and price ranges.

Resorts and Hotels

1. Luxurious Resorts: Wisconsin has an excellent selection of opulent resorts that are situated in beautiful landscapes. These resorts provide sumptuous facilities and first-rate service, from the American Club in Kohler, renowned for its world-class golf courses and spa, to The Osthoff Resort in Elkhart Lake, with its picturesque lakeside setting.

2. Historic Hotels: Spend your time in one of Wisconsin's historic hotels to fully immerse yourself in the past. A well-known landmark in Milwaukee, the Pfister Hotel is renowned for its grandeur and art collection. Arbour Vitae's Red Crown Lodge provides a traditional Northwoods experience.

3. Boutique Hotels: Look for boutique hotels that offer individualized service in distinctive settings. The Charmant in La Crosse emanates French-inspired beauty, while the Iron Horse Hotel in Milwaukee caters to motorcyclists.

4. Family-Friendly Accommodations: Wisconsin has a large number of family-friendly hotels and resorts. For instance, the Great Wolf Lodge in Wisconsin Dells features themed rooms and an indoor waterpark. There are several family-friendly activities available at the Wilderness Resort in the Dells.

5. Beachfront Retreats: Wisconsin has a lot of lakes, which makes it possible to find lovely beachfront lodging. The Heidel House Resort on Green Lake mixes peace and activities, while Lake Geneva provides waterfront accommodations with breathtaking views.

6. Golf Resorts: Golf resorts abound, including Whistling Straits at Destination Kohler and The

American Club in Kohler, all of which are known for their championship golf courses.

7. Ski Resorts: For people who like winter activities, ski resorts like Granite Peak in Wausau provide comfortable lodging near the slopes.

Other Facilities:

- **Spas:** A lot of Wisconsin resorts include full-service spas that provide visitors with ways to unwind and revitalize.
- **Dining:** The state's culinary characteristics are frequently highlighted in the on-site dining options, which vary from fine dining to casual cuisine.
- **Activities:** Depending on the resort, you can have access to nearby hiking trails, golf courses, waterparks, and more.
- **Event Facilities:** Several resorts provide the tools necessary to hold conferences, weddings, and other events, making them adaptable alternatives for all types of visitors.

- **Pet-Friendly Accommodations:** If you're traveling with a furry companion, Wisconsin has

hotels and resorts that accept your four-legged family members.

The hotels and resorts in Wisconsin offer welcoming accommodations and wonderful vacations to a range of tourists. You'll discover the ideal lodging to suit your Wisconsin travels, whether you're looking for luxury and leisure, fun family activities, adventure, or historic charm.

Cozy Cottages and Cabins

In the middle of the state's stunning natural surroundings, Wisconsin provides a wide selection of cozy cabins and cottages if you're seeking a more private and intimate experience. These lodgings offer a sense of privacy and a chance to unplug from the busyness of daily life.

1. Northwoods Retreats: The state of Wisconsin's north is home to a variety of quaint cabins and cottages that are tucked away in the middle of the Northwoods. These lodgings frequently have lakes and forests around them, providing a tranquil haven.

2. Door County Cottages: Door County has charming cottages with views of Lake Michigan or Green Bay, as well as scenic shorelines and landscapes. It's the best place to go on a romantic weekend getaway.

3. Rustic Cabins: If you're looking for a rustic adventure, check out a cabin in the Nicolet National Forest or Chequamegon-Nicolet National Forest for a genuine taste of the great outdoors.

4. Lakeside Charm: Cabins and cottages on the water's edge abound throughout Wisconsin, giving the state its lakeside charm. Fans of fishing, boating, and water activities will love these accommodations.

5. Cosy Fires: Many cabins include warm fires, which makes them the perfect option for a winter getaway. Picture yourself enjoying a cup of hot chocolate by the fire while watching the snow fall outside.

RV parks and campgrounds

There are many possibilities for camping in Wisconsin if you want to get closer to the natural world. There is something for every camping aficionado, from classic campsites to fully furnished RV parks.

1. State Parks: Wisconsin's state parks provide camping options so you may spend time in the great outdoors. Make a campground reservation and take advantage of camping, hiking, and fishing.

2. RV Parks: A network of RV parks with hookups, showers, and other amenities are available to RV lovers. These parks are frequently located close to important landmarks and scenic delights.

3. Rustic Camping: Wisconsin's national forests provide the chance for backcountry camping, where you may fully immerse yourself in nature, for a genuinely tough experience.

Unique Accommodations: Treehouses and Lighthouses

Lighthouses and treehouses are just two of the unusual lodging options Wisconsin has to offer visitors looking for really one-of-a-kind experiences.

1. Lighthouse Stays: The North Point Lighthouse in Milwaukee or the Cana Island Lighthouse in Door County are two examples of antique lighthouses where you may stay. These distinctive lodgings offer spectacular views and history.

2. Treehouse Getaways: People are increasingly using treehouses as a means to get back in touch with nature. In Wisconsin, several treehouse lodgings let you rest comfortably and stylishly among the trees.

3. Safari Tents: A few Wisconsin vacation spots offer safari tent lodging, which combines the excitement of camping with more comfort and elegance.

4. Historic Inns: Wisconsin is home to several exquisite bed & breakfasts and historic inns that offer a distinctive and individualized hotel experience.

Wisconsin provides a wide variety of lodging options to improve your trip experience, whether you prefer the cozy appeal of cabins, the independence of camping, or the novelty of lighthouse and treehouse stays. You may experience the state's distinctive culture and natural beauty via each choice.

Chapter 5: Dining and Culinary Delights

The culinary heritage of Wisconsin is a lovely fusion of warm, familiar, and various flavors. Your trip to Wisconsin must include experiencing the state's rich culinary tradition.

Wisconsin's Culinary Traditions

1. Cheese and Dairy Products: Wisconsin's cheese is the state's culinary signature. The state is renowned as America's Dairyland and produces cheeses that have won awards. Make sure to enjoy traditional foods like curds, Swiss, and cheddar. On cheese trails, don't forget to stop at cheese factories and creameries to learn more about the production of cheese.

2. Bratwurst: Wisconsin is the home of bratwurst, which you really must try. Enjoy these delectable sausages, which are frequently paired with sauerkraut and mustard, at neighborhood restaurants or summertime festivals.

3. Friday Fish Fry: Fish fries are a Friday night institution in Wisconsin. Fish is served in restaurants, supper clubs, and pubs. It is frequently served with coleslaw, rye bread, and potato pancakes.

4. Kringle: Give your taste buds a treat by indulging in this favorite Wisconsin dessert that originated as a Danish pastry. Visit a bakery to try a piece of this delicious, flaky treat.

5. Beer and Brandy Old Fashioned: The beer and brandy old fashioned is a Wisconsin-specific variation on the traditional drink. A basic whisky Old Fashioned, a brandy Old Fashioned, or a brandy Sweet Old Fashioned are all options.

6. Frozen Custard: Indulge in frozen custard, Wisconsin's take on ice cream. Both residents and visitors love this creamy, decadent treat.

Cheese Trails and Dairy Destinations

1. Cheese Trails: Visit nearby cheese producers while on a cheese trail excursion, such as the Dairylands Best Cheese Tour. You will have the opportunity to try and buy a broad range of cheeses, including the well-known squeaky cheese curds.

2. Dairy Farms: Wisconsin's dairy farms offer an insight into the world of dairy farming. You may view cows, observe the milking procedure, and sample fresh dairy products on several farms that provide tours to guests.

3. Cheese Festivals: To celebrate all things cheese, go to cheese festivals like the Cheese Curd Festival in Ellsworth or the Wisconsin Cheese Festival in Little Chute.

Farm-to-Table Dining

1. Farmers' Markets: Try seasonal, fresh food, handmade goods, and sweets at your neighborhood farmers' market. One of the biggest and most well-known in the state is the Dane County Farmers' Market in Madison.

2. Farm-to-Table Restaurants: Locally sourced products are used at Wisconsin's farm-to-table restaurants, which are located there. These places provide a dining experience that emphasizes the area's finest, seasonal products.

3. Culinary Excursions: Take part in farm and food excursions, like the Door County Farm Tour, to learn more about the regional food scene and savor delectable farm-fresh fare.

Wineries and Craft Breweries

1. Brewery Tours: The craft beer industry in Wisconsin is flourishing. Visit breweries and try a variety of beers, including IPAs and stouts. Craft breweries may be found in great numbers in cities like Milwaukee and Madison.

2. Wineries and Vineyards: Discover Wisconsin's vineyards and wineries, which make premium wines from grapes that can withstand the cold. Wine lovers will love the Door County Wine Trail and the Great River Road Wine Trail.

3. Beer and Wine Festivals: Attend festivals like the Great Taste of the Midwest in Madison or the Kohler Food and Wine Experience in Kohler to experience the thriving beer and wine culture.

Wisconsin's agricultural legacy is strongly ingrained in its culinary traditions, which also demonstrate the state's dedication to using only the best, locally produced resources. Wisconsin's culinary scene guarantees a feast for your senses, whether you're delighting in cheese and dairy treats, savoring farm-fresh cuisine, or toasting with craft beers and local wines.

Chapter 6: Outdoor Adventures

With a vast network of hiking and bicycling trails, Wisconsin's varied landscapes provide a variety of options for outdoor lovers. These routes let you see the state's natural beauty up close.

Biking Trails and Hiking

1. Ice Age Trail: The approximately 1,000-mile Ice Age Trail, one of the state's crown treasures, traces the route of the previous Ice Age. Hikers may go through a variety of segments, each of which offers distinctive geological characteristics, such as glacier formations and tranquil woodlands.

2. Kettle Moraine State Forest: This state park in eastern Wisconsin has several hiking and biking paths for people of all ability levels. The stunning lakes and undulating topography of the woodland provide for a beautiful outdoor experience.

3. Chequamegon-Nicolet National Forest: The Chequamegon-Nicolet National Forest is located in northern Wisconsin and has a vast network of hiking and mountain biking trails. On miles of pristine paths, explore forests, rivers, and lakes.

4. Devil's Lake State Park: From its quartzite bluffs, Devil's Lake State Park offers strenuous treks and breathtaking vistas. There are several routes available for hikers, including ones that round the park's famous lake.

5. Mountain Biking Trails: Mountain biking is becoming more and more popular in Wisconsin. Riders will find challenging terrain and breathtaking scenery on Cable's CAMBA (Chequamegon Area Mountain Bike Association) trails.

6. Rails-to-Trails: Wisconsin also offers a vast network of rail trails, or former railway lines that have been transformed into beautiful bike and hiking routes. One excellent example is the Elroy-Sparta State Trail, which has recognizable tunnels.

Water Sports: Kayaking, Canoeing, and Fishing

1. Wisconsin River: From calm glides to exhilarating whitewater portions, the Wisconsin River offers a variety of paddling experiences. Its winding path may be explored by kayakers and canoers.

2. Lake Superior: The Apostle Islands in this body of water provide fantastic possibilities for sea kayaking. Paddle through unspoiled beaches, sandstone caverns, and the breathtaking Apostle Islands.

3. Fishing: Wisconsin is a fishing haven because of its many lakes and rivers. The state offers fishing opportunities for all skill levels, whether you choose to cast for muskies in Hayward or fish for trout in streams in the Driftless Area.

4. Fly Fishing: The Driftless Area is a hotspot for fly fishers. It is renowned for its spring-fed rivers and waters that are rich in limestone, providing a great challenge for trout.

Winter Sports: Skiing and Snowmobiling

1. Skiing: Wisconsin is a winter sports enthusiast's paradise. Choose between cross-country skiing on miles of groomed paths in parks and woods or downhill skiing at resorts like Granite Peak near Wausau.

2. Snowmobiling: Wisconsin is home to a vast network of snowmobile trails that cover hundreds of kilometers. Snowmobile across the Northwoods, stopping at inviting resorts along the route.

3. Ice Fishing: Ice fishing has become a well-liked wintertime activity. On frozen lakes like Lake Winnebago, set up an ice shack and try your hand at capturing perch, walleye, and panfish.

4. Winter Festivals: To commemorate the season, many Wisconsin municipalities have winter festivals that feature ice skating, snow sculpture competitions, and other events.

The outdoor activities in Wisconsin are suitable for a variety of reasons and interests. The state's various landscapes are your playground for year-round outdoor activity, whether you're hiking or bicycling in the summer months, kayaking and fishing on pristine lakes, or savoring the rush of skiing and snowmobiling in the winter.

Chapter 7: Family-Friendly Fun

Wisconsin is the perfect place for a fun-filled family vacation since it has a wide variety of amusement parks and waterparks that promise exhilarating rides, family-friendly entertainment, and refreshing aquatic activities.

Waterparks and Amusement Parks

1. Wisconsin Dells: Known as the "Waterpark Capital of the World," Wisconsin Dells is the location of an incredible variety of waterparks, including Noah's Ark Waterpark, the largest waterpark in the country. There are several kid-friendly slides, wave pools, and lazy rivers available. Visit Mt. Olympus Water and Theme Park or the Kalahari Resort, which mixes water and theme park activities, for amusement park enjoyment.

2. Bay Beach Amusement Park: This Green Bay attraction is a pleasant, cost-effective vacation spot. Families may enjoy a playground, a picturesque picnic area, and vintage rides such as the Zippin Pippin roller coaster.

3. Six Flags Great America: Located in Gurnee, Illinois, just across the border from Illinois, this theme park features exciting roller coasters and kid-friendly attractions for an exhilarating experience.

4. Timbavati Wildlife Park: The Wisconsin Dells neighborhood's Timbavati Wildlife Park blends the features of an amusement park with a wildlife park. Families may take part in animal interactions and discover a variety of international animals.

5. Noah's Ark Waterpark: As one of the biggest waterparks in the world, Noah's Ark has thrill rides, wave pools, and tranquil float excursions that are appropriate for people of all ages.

6. The Wilds of Asia at the Milwaukee County Zoo: The Milwaukee County Zoo is well known for its zoo, but it also has a section that is similar to an amusement park called The Wilds of Asia. After seeing the zoo's animal displays, kids may enjoy the rides and other activities here.

Animal Encounters at Zoos

1. Milwaukee County Zoo: More than 2,000 animals from all around the world may be found in the Milwaukee County Zoo. Visitors may experience animal interactions, explore exotic species, and learn about conservation initiatives.

2. Henry Vilas Zoo: This free zoo is located in Madison and is excellent for family activities. It includes a wide range of creatures, such as huge cats, primates, and birds.

3. Green Bay's NEW Zoo & Adventure Park: This zoo blends animal displays with action-packed activities like zip-lining and a ropes course.

Science Centres and Children's Museums

1. Betty Brinn Children's Museum: Located in Milwaukee, the Betty Brinn Children's Museum is a great location for families since it provides interactive exhibits, seminars, and educational programs.

2. Madison Children's Museum: The Madison Children's Museum offers interactive exhibitions, kid-friendly art studios, and fun kid-oriented events.

3. Discovery World: Situated near Milwaukee on the beaches of Lake Michigan, Discovery World is a science and technology museum with educational opportunities for people of all ages, interactive displays, and an aquarium.

The many family-friendly activities that Wisconsin's theme parks, waterparks, zoos, and children's museums provide offer a wide variety of entertainment and education. These locations provide families a chance to connect, educate themselves, and make lifelong memories.

Chapter 8: Culture and The Arts

Numerous museums and historical sites in Wisconsin highlight the state's rich cultural heritage and varied history. These places provide an intriguing voyage through history, art, and the distinctive tales that have created the state.

Historical and Museum Locations

1. The Wisconsin Historical Society Museum, which is in Madison, is the best place to learn about Wisconsin's past. It offers informative programs, artifacts, and immersive exhibitions that illuminate the state's past.

2. EAA Aviation Museum: Located in Oshkosh, the EAA Aviation Museum allows visitors to learn about aviation through interactive displays, antique aircraft, and aviation artifacts.

3. Pendarvis Historic Site: The Pendarvis Historic Site at Mineral Point lets you travel back in time to the early 19th century when Cornish immigrants first colonized the area. Investigate the structures that have been preserved and discover the region's mining history.

4. Old World Wisconsin: This living history museum in Eagle has more than 50 19th-century structures. Through interactive displays and costumed interpreters, it provides a distinctive look into Wisconsin's agricultural and immigration heritage.

5. H.H. Bennett Studio & Museum: Situated in Wisconsin Dells, this museum honors the life and work of H.H. Bennett, a famous photographer of the late 19th and early 20th centuries known for his iconic photographs of the Dells. View his beautiful pictures while exploring his studio.

The National Railroad Museum is located in Green Bay, where you may learn about the country's railroading history. Discover a sizable collection of trains, exhibitions, and engines.

Performing Arts and Art Galleries

1. Milwaukee Art Museum: The Milwaukee Art Museum is a marvel of architecture and is distinguished by its recognizable "wings." You'll discover a varied collection of artwork there, ranging from ancient to modern, including pieces by well-known painters like Georgia O'Keeffe.

2. Chazen Museum of Art: The Chazen Museum of Art, which is situated at the University of Wisconsin–Madison, is home to a sizable collection of artworks, including works by European, American, and Asian artists. Special exhibitions and educational events are held there.

3. John Michael Kohler Arts Centre: Located in Sheboygan, this venue for the arts features recurring exhibitions of modern art. It is also renowned for its creative bathrooms, each of which was created by a different artist.

4. Overture Centre for the Arts: The Overture Centre in Madison serves as the city's main hub for performing arts. Ballet, Broadway plays, concerts, and a variety of other live entertainment are presented there.

5. American Players Theatre: This amphitheatre-style outdoor theatre group, located near Spring Green, offers superb productions of both classic and modern plays.

6. The Sharon Lynne Wilson Centre for the Arts, which is situated in Brookfield, provides a variety of cultural events, including performances of classical music and exhibitions of visual arts.

The state's rich history, from its immigrant origins to its significance in the creation of aviation and railroads, may be explored through Wisconsin's museums and historic sites. On the other hand, you may immerse yourself in creative and cultural expression in art galleries and performance spaces. The arts and cultural sector in Wisconsin has something to offer everyone, whether they are looking for historical insights or creative inspiration.

Chapter 9: Festivals & Events

Wisconsin is a state that knows how to party, and you can find a broad variety of festivals and events that appeal to a wide range of interests and preferences throughout the year.

The Year-Round Festivals in Wisconsin

1. Summer Festivals: A flurry of outdoor festivities take place during the pleasant summer months. "The World's Largest Music Festival," Summerfest in Milwaukee, features live music, food, and entertainment. For fans of aviation, the EAA AirVenture Oshkosh is a must-attend event. Don't miss Milwaukee's Indian Summer Festival, which honors Native American culture, for a cultural experience.

2. Autumn Harvest Festivals: With the arrival of autumn, Wisconsin comes alive with these events.

Throughout the state, apple and pumpkin festivals are hosted where you may select your fruit, sip cider, and navigate corn mazes. An original way to celebrate the cranberry harvest is at the Warrens Cranberry Festival.

3. Winter Wonderland: Wisconsin's winters are filled with entrancing celebrations. A must-see attraction is the Lake Geneva Ice Castles, a glacial paradise. A celebration of winter sports, the Sturgeon Spectacular in Fond du Lac includes activities like ice fishing and snow sculpture. Visit the Oshkosh Celebration of Lights for a spectacular holiday experience.

4. Spring Blooms: Wisconsin welcomes the rebirth of the natural world as springtime approaches. The beautiful sandstone formations that have made the area renowned are on display during the Wisconsin Dells Dells Boat Tours. A cinephile's paradise, the Wisconsin Film Festival in Madison showcases indie films and documentaries.

5. Cultural Events: You may immerse yourself in Wisconsin's diverse cultural history at various times of the year. Milwaukee holds German Fest to recognize the significant German impact on the state. The Waukesha Highland Games are an energetic celebration of Scottish culture. A magnificent event where you may learn about Native American customs is the Lac du Flambeau Pow-Wow.

Important Dates Calendar

1. Fourth-of-July Celebrations: Wisconsin's villages and communities put on amazing Fourth-of-July celebrations with parades, fireworks, and patriotic music. Don't miss Madison's fireworks over Lake Monona or Green Bay's FreedomFest.

2. Door County Cherry Festival: This celebration of the cherry harvest, which takes place in July, has a parade, an arts and crafts fair, live music, and tasty cuisine with cherry themes.

3. Bratwurst Days: Sheboygan, the 'Bratwurst Capital of the World', holds this event where you can savor this flavorful sausage while taking part in live entertainment and family-friendly activities.

4. Oktoberfest: La Crosse has one of the biggest Oktoberfests in the country, complete with parades, live music, beer tents, and authentic German food.

5. EAA AirVenture Oshkosh: The largest aviation event in the world, EAA AirVenture, draws visitors from all over the world. It offers airshows, demonstrations of aircraft, and educational activities.

6. The Holidazzle Parade, A cherished Christmas event in downtown Milwaukee, features Santa Claus as well as lit floats, marching bands, and other festive characters.

7. Musky Festival: This fishing-themed festival in Hayward features a joyous procession, live music, and the coronation of the "Musky Queen."

Everybody may enjoy Wisconsin's year-round celebrations, which range from cuisine and the great outdoors to music and culture. No matter when you decide to come to Wisconsin, you're likely to discover a celebration or event that will make your trip even more enjoyable.

Chapter 10: Practical Information

A smooth and comfortable trip will be ensured by being prepared with travel advice and safety precautions. Traveling to Wisconsin is an exciting experience.

Safety Advice for Travel

1. Weather Awareness: Wisconsin has a variety of weather patterns. Winters bring chilly temperatures and snow, while summers may be hot and muggy. Check the weather forecast and be ready with the proper attire.

2. Safety Precautions: Wisconsin is often a safe place to visit, but it's crucial to exercise common sense when it comes to safety. Particularly in metropolitan locations, secure your possessions, lock your vehicle, and pay attention to your surroundings.

3. Safety and Health: Wisconsin has first-rate medical facilities, but it's a good idea to obtain travel insurance that includes coverage for unexpected medical expenses. Verify your immunization records and have any essential drugs on hand if you have allergies.

4. Driving Safety: If you intend to hire a car, get acquainted with the local traffic laws. Always buckle up, drive under the speed limit, and never use a phone while driving.

5. Wildlife Interactions: Be cautious of potential wildlife interactions when visiting natural places. Even though Wisconsin's wildlife is often not hostile, stay your distance and avoid feeding it.

6. Emergency Contact: Save emergency phone numbers in your phone, such as 911, for quick assistance. Just in case, make a note of the embassy or consulate's contact details.

Packing Advice

1. Clothes: Pack a range of clothes depending on the season. Winters call for warm layers, while summers call for light, breathable apparel. Keep a pair of supportive walking shoes on hand.

2. Outdoor Gear: Bring hiking boots, rain gear, and any necessary camping gear if you intend to experience Wisconsin's natural splendor.

3. Electronics: Bring your phone, camera, and chargers for electronics. For longer outdoor trips, think about getting a power bank.

4. Travel Documents: Take your passport, license, and any required visas with you. These records should be duplicated and then kept in separate storage.

5. Medication: Make sure you have a sufficient supply if you take prescription drugs. Carry a compact first-aid kit that includes basic supplies like bandages and painkillers.

6. Currency: Wisconsin accepts US dollars as payment. For convenience, keep some cash on hand in addition to credit and debit cards.

7. Travel Adapters: Wisconsin employs Type A and Type B electrical outlets. Depending on your native country, a travel adaptor could be required.

Maps and Navigation

1. Smartphone Apps: For simple navigation, download Google Maps or Apple Maps before your journey. They offer traffic alerts and real-time instructions.

2. Physical Maps: If you want to travel through remote locations with spotty cell coverage, bring a physical road map or atlas.

3. GPS Devices: Bring a portable GPS with current maps if you prefer dedicated GPS navigation.

4. Wi-Fi and Data: Check to see whether your phone plan covers data usage for navigation and map apps. If you often go abroad, ask your carrier about roaming possibilities.

5. Landmarks and Signage: Pay attention to landmarks and signage on the roads. The road signs in Wisconsin are often easy to read and useful for navigation.

6. Visitor information centers: are a great place to find maps, brochures, and suggestions from knowledgeable locals. They may offer helpful direction for your path.

Wisconsin has a wide range of things to offer, from urban exploration to outdoor pursuits. You may get the most out of your trip to Wisconsin and produce priceless memories by following travel advice, staying safe, packing sensibly, and using navigational equipment.

Chapter 11: Hidden Gems and Local Tips

Wisconsin has several well-known sights and places, but there are also many undiscovered wonders and off-the-beaten-path adventures just waiting for you to explore. These lesser-known gems offer a distinctive and genuine view of the state.

Off-the-Beaten-Track Excursions

1. Apostle Islands Ice Caverns: These ice caverns, which may be found near Bayfield, are a winter paradise. You may explore the surreal ice formations within the sea caves when Lake Superior freezes over.

2. Cave of the Mounds: This natural limestone cave close to Blue Mounds was stumbled upon in the 1930s and is a subterranean marvel. It is a hidden geological jewel due to its stalactites, stalagmites, and distinctive rock formations.

3. High Cliff State Park: This park, which is located on the eastern border of Lake Winnebago, has hiking trails, limestone cliffs, and breathtaking vistas. It's a more sedate option to the more known state parks.

4. Frank Lloyd Wright's Wyoming Valley School: The lesser-known Wyoming Valley School, which was built by Frank Lloyd Wright, is located in Spring Green. It serves as a monument to the talent of the great architect and is accessible for tourists.

5. Rustic Roads: Wisconsin is home to a network of picturesque roads known as "Rustic Roads." These little-used roads provide beautiful drives across the countryside.

6. Ferry Bluff Rock Formations: Visit the Ferry Bluff State Natural Area, close to Sauk City, to see the old rock formations that line the Wisconsin River. For hikers and wildlife lovers, it is a secret gem.

Local Favourites

Following the advice of locals who are intimately familiar with the place is among the finest methods to have a genuine travel experience.

1. Culver's ButterBurgers and Frozen Custard: This local fast food company is a favorite among residents for its creamy frozen custard and buttery burgers. Try a "Concrete Mixer" with your preferred mix-ins as well.

2. Fish Fry Fridays: Wisconsinites adore the custom of Friday fish fries. Go for a hefty platter of battered fish, coleslaw, and rye bread at a neighborhood pub or supper club.

3. Door County Cherry Pie: Enjoy a piece of cherry pie prepared with fruits harvested in Door County while you're there. It's a delectable delicacy that perfectly encapsulates the spirit of the place.

4. Friday Night Fish Boils: You may take part in a traditional fish boil in communities like the Door Peninsula, especially in the village of Fish Creek.

Observe as a great cook makes a feast of whitefish from Lake Michigan, potatoes, and onions.

5. Supper Clubs: A traditional Wisconsin eating experience is a supper club. Locals go to these inviting spots for drinks, relish platters, and traditional Wisconsin fare. A well-liked drink is the Old-Fashioned.

6. Hiking the Ice Age Trail: Local outdoor enthusiasts love to hike the Ice Age Trail. Residents of Wisconsin take delight in visiting the state's many regions, from gently undulating farmlands to pristine woods.

7. Lambeau Field tailgating: If you're in Green Bay during the football season, join locals for a pre-game tailgate party at the Green Bay Packers home stadium. It's a custom that is well embedded in the culture of the area.

8. Door County Wineries: Door County is well-known for its cherry orchards, but it also has several top-notch wineries. Local favorites include Simon Creek Vineyard & Winery and Lautenbach's Orchard Country Winery.

9. Camping in the Northwoods: For a genuine feeling of the great outdoors, camp among locals in places like the Northern Highland-American Legion State Forest or the Chequamegon-Nicolet National Forest.

10. Brandy Old Fashioned: Popular among Wisconsin residents, this cocktail is known as the state drink. Enjoy it in the neighborhood bars and nightclubs.

You can discover activities and locations not listed in travel guides by paying attention to locals' advice. It's a chance to get to know Wisconsin's true character and learn about the treasures that its people hold dear.

Chapter 12: Beyond Wisconsin

While Wisconsin has many attractions, exploring nearby states might broaden your trip options. Day travels to nearby states provide a wonderful chance to encounter a variety of environments, cultures, and experiences.

Day Trips to Neighboring States

1. Chicago, Illinois: Chicago is a renowned city renowned for its architecture, art, and culinary culture. It is situated just south of the Wisconsin-Illinois border. You may visit well-known locations including Navy Pier, Millennium Park, and the Art Institute of Chicago. At Wrigley Field, enjoy deep-dish pizza while watching a Cubs game.

2. Minneapolis-Saint Paul, Minnesota: Western Wisconsin can easily travel to the Twin

Cities of Minneapolis and Saint Paul. Enjoy a variety of cultural landmarks, such as the Cathedral of Saint Paul, the Mall of America, and the Minneapolis Institute of Art. The region is particularly well-known for its vast park system and stunning lakes.

3. Dubuque, Iowa: Travel over the Mississippi River to this quaint waterfront city. Visit the National Mississippi River Museum and Aquarium, ride the Fenelon Place Elevator, or enjoy a paddlewheel boat tour of the river.

4. Door County, Wisconsin: This Wisconsin destination is worth noting as a day trip from the state's largest cities even though it officially falls within the state. It provides a distinctive escape inside the state and is well known for its scenic beauty, quaint towns, and waterfront activities.

5. Lake Geneva, Wisconsin: This popular day trip location in southeast Wisconsin is noted for its picturesque lakeside environment, old houses, and outdoor pursuits like boating and hiking.

Combining the Great Lakes

The Superior, Michigan, and Lake Michigan basins of the Great Lakes encircle Wisconsin's northern border. Whether you are in Wisconsin or ready to go outside of the state, these extraordinary bodies of water provide chances for exploration and leisure.

1. Apostle Islands, Lake Superior: The Apostle Islands, a series of 22 islands just off the northern Wisconsin shore, are home to sea caves, lighthouses, and unspoiled nature. Take the ferry from Bayfield, Wisconsin, and spend the day exploring the island.

2. Traverse City, Michigan: This lakefront city in Michigan is renowned for its breathtaking beaches, cherry orchards, and wineries. It's a terrific location for a day of wine tasting and beachcombing.

3. Sleeping Bear Dunes National Lakeshore, Michigan: This national lakeshore is located just north of Traverse City and features large dunes, hiking paths, and stunning vistas of Lake Michigan. To get a different perspective of the lake, climb the dunes.

4. Mackinac Island, Michigan: A car-free vacation spot with a charming history, Mackinac Island is reachable by boat from Mackinaw City, Michigan. Discover the Victorian architecture, ride a bicycle around the island, and indulge in the local fudge.

5. Grand Marais, Minnesota: Located on the northern side of Lake Superior, Grand Marais is a charming community with a creative energy. Explore the Superior National Forest on foot, stop by the North House Folk School, or just take in the breathtaking lake views.

6. Indiana Dunes, Indiana: Indiana Dunes National Park, which is located just beyond the southernmost point of Lake Michigan, has a diversified terrain made up of dunes, woods, and marshes. It's a special place to go trekking, birding, and going to the beach.

7. Door County, Wisconsin: Although it is technically in Wisconsin, exploring the Great Lakes is perfectly complemented by Door County's coastline splendor along Lake Michigan and Green

Bay. Enjoy water sports, beautiful lighthouses, and scenic roads.

A wide range of leisure options and breathtaking scenery may be found in the Great Lakes. There is plenty to discover outside of Wisconsin, whether you are drawn to the untamed majesty of Lake Superior or the quaint cities along Lake Michigan. Your vacation experience may be enhanced and you can make enduring memories by taking day excursions or staying longer in these nearby regions.

Conclusion

Now that your trip across Wisconsin is coming to an end, it's time to say goodbye to the Badger State. This summary reflects your travels while also recognizing Wisconsin's natural splendor, rich culture, and welcoming nature.

A Heartfelt Goodbye to Wisconsin

1. Recollections to Treasure: Wisconsin unquestionably made an imprint on your travel-related recollections. You have encountered a kaleidoscope of experiences that will stay with you for the rest of your life, whether it is the breathtaking views of the Door Peninsula, the busy streets of Milwaukee, or the tranquil woodlands of the Northwoods.

2. Gastronomic Joys: From cheese curds to Friday night fish fries and Brandy Old Fashioneds, you've enjoyed the gastronomic joys of Wisconsin's traditions. The flavor of these regional specialties will stay with you long after you depart.

3. Local Kindness: Your trip has unquestionably been made more pleasant by Wisconsin residents' warmth and kindness. The kindness of the inhabitants has made Wisconsin feel like a home away from home, whether you've engaged with them at a dinner club, a family-run dairy farm, or a lakeside resort.

4. Natural Beauty: You've been treated to a visual feast by Wisconsin's varied landscapes, which range from rolling farmlands to towering bluffs and clear lakes. Your senses have been aroused by this state's magnificence, and you now have a keen appreciation for nature.

5. Cultural Riches: By visiting museums, historical landmarks, and the arts and culture sector, you were able to learn more about Wisconsin's colorful past and present. You leave with a richer awareness of the history of the state.

6. Adventure and Tranquillity: Whether you're drawn to Great Lakes tranquility, outdoor excursions in state parks, or festival excitement, Wisconsin boasts the ideal mix of experiences. You have been able to create your own story of the state because of this dynamic range.

7. Hidden Jewels and Beyond: Your travels to other states and hidden jewels have extended your perspective and made you see that Wisconsin is only one piece of a much broader tapestry of beauty. You've found that every part of this area has a distinctive tale to tell.

Take the memories, pictures, and friendships you made along the trip with you as you say Wisconsin farewell. Keep in mind the peaceful times spent by the lakes, the joyous celebrations, and the breathtaking beauty of nature. Your trip to Wisconsin is a chapter in your life's experience; it will always be characterized by happy recollections and the desire to visit this amazing state once more.

So until we cross paths again, I bid you farewell and thank you for the unique experiences you gave me, promising to always treasure the memories.

Appendix

Useful Resources

It's crucial to have access to useful tools when traveling in Wisconsin since they may improve your experience, give aid in case of an emergency, and answer your questions on where to go. A list of these resources is provided in the appendix to make your journey as easy as possible.

1. Wisconsin Department of Tourism: For thorough information on attractions, events, lodging options, and travel suggestions, visit the official website at https://www.travelwisconsin.com. Your starting point for organizing an effective trip to Wisconsin is this resource.

2. Travel Wisconsin Mobile App: Download the official Travel Wisconsin mobile app (available for iOS and Android) to access travel information, such as event listings, lodging options, and directions, while you're on the go.

3. Wisconsin State Parks: Visit the Wisconsin Department of Natural Resources website (https://dnr.wisconsin.gov/topic/parks) for details on state parks, including camping reservations, maps, and activities.

4. Wisconsin Historical Society: Visit the Wisconsin Historical Society's website (https://www.wisconsinhistory.org/) to learn more about the state's extensive history. Find out about historical landmarks, museums, and learning tools.

5. Wisconsin Department of Transportation: Visit the WisDOT Website (https://wisconsindot.gov/Pages/home.aspx) for up-to-date information on construction, road conditions, and traffic.

Contact details

1. Emergency Services: Call 911 for urgent assistance in case of an emergency. In all of

Wisconsin, the emergency services line is open around the clock.

2. Local Law Enforcement: Get in touch with the local law enforcement office in the region you're visiting if you need non-emergency police help or to report a small incident.

3. Medical Assistance: Find the closest hospital or medical institution if you require medical attention or have any worries about your health. The healthcare system in Wisconsin is first-rate.

Tourist Information Centers

1. Wisconsin Welcome Centres: Located at several points of entry into the state, these facilities provide travelers with maps, pamphlets, and useful information.

2. Local Visitor Bureaus: Local visitor bureaus or tourism offices may be found in the majority of popular tourist attractions and towns. These resources might provide you with recommendations, maps, and information particular to the region.

3. Rest Stations: To help travelers plan their trips, Wisconsin's rest stations frequently offer information kiosks with pamphlets and maps.

4. Airports: Major international airports with helpful employees and visitor information desks include Milwaukee Mitchell International Airport and Dane County Regional Airport in Madison.

It is a good idea to double-check the authenticity and availability of these resources before and during your journey because information and contact details might change over time. Having access to these tools guarantees that you'll be well-prepared and able to complete your Wisconsin journey. Travel safely!

Index

Detailed Index for Quick Reference

This index offers a thorough list of the subjects, locations, and important details covered in the "Wisconsin Travel Guide" for quick and easy reference. This index will make it easy for you to search the guide for certain locations, things to do, or helpful tips.

A

- Accommodations
- Hotels and Resorts
- Cosy Cabins and Cottages
- Unique Stays: Lighthouses and Treehouses
- Amusement Parks and Waterparks
- Apostle Islands
- Apostle Islands Adventure

B

- Bayfield
- Apostle Islands Adventure
- Freshwater Fishing Paradise
- Beyond Wisconsin
- Combining with the Great Lakes
- Brandy Old Fashioned
- Budgeting for Your Wisconsin Adventure

C

- Cave of the Mounds
- Cheese Trails and Dairy Destinations
- Chicago, Illinois
- Culinary Delights
- Cheese Trails and Dairy Destinations
- Craft Breweries and Wineries
- Farm-to-Table Dining
- Culture
- Museums and Historic Sites
- Performing Arts

D

- Day Trips to Neighboring States
- Dining and Culinary Delights
- Cheese Trails and Dairy Destinations

- Craft Breweries and Wineries
- Wisconsin's Culinary Traditions
- Door County
  - Door County Cherry Pie
  - Door County Wineries

E .
- Emergency Services
- Exploring Wisconsin's Regions
- Central Wisconsin
- Northern Wisconsin
- Southern Wisconsin

F
- Family-Friendly Fun
- Amusement Parks and Waterparks
- Children's Museums and Science Centers
- Zoos and Wildlife Encounters
- Festivals and Events
- Key Events Calendar
- Wisconsin's Year-Round Festivities

G
- Green County
- Swiss Heritage

H

- Hiking and Biking Trails
- Hidden Gems and Local Tips
- Locals' Favorites
- Off the Beaten Path Adventures
- Historic Sites
- Museums and Historic Sites
- Hotels and Resorts

I

- Indian Summer Festival
- Introduction

K

- Key Events Calendar

L

- Lake Geneva
- Lake Geneva, Wisconsin
- Local Favorites
- Locals' Favorites

M

- Madison

- The Capital Experience
- Maps and Navigation
- Milwaukee
- Brew City Delights
- Minneapolis-Saint Paul, Minnesota
- Museums and Historic Sites

N
- National Railroad Museum
- Northern Highland-American Legion State Forest
- Northern Wisconsin
- Navigating the Roadways
- Neighboring States
- Day Trips to Neighboring States
- North House Folk School

O
- Oshkosh
- The EAA AirVenture Oshkosh
- Outdoor Adventures
- Hiking and Biking Trails
- Water Sports: Kayaking, Canoeing, and Fishing
- Winter Sports: Skiing and Snowmobiling

P

- Packing Guide
- Practical Information
- Travel Tips and Safety
- Planning Your Trip
- Setting Your Itinerary
- Pendarvis Historic Site

R
- Rock Formations of Ferry Bluff
- Rustic Roads

S
- Setting Your Itinerary
- Sleeping Bear Dunes National Lakeshore, Michigan
- Southern Wisconsin
- St. Croix National Scenic Riverway
- Stevens Point
- Arts and Culture
- Sturgeon Spectacular
- Supper Clubs

T
- Tourist Information Centers
- Traverse City, Michigan

- Travel Guide
- Travel Tips and Safety
- Travel Wisconsin Mobile App
- Traveling to Wisconsin
- Transportation Options

U
- Useful Resources

W
- Warrens Cranberry Festival
- Weather Awareness
- Wisconsin Dells
- Waterpark Capital of the World
- Wisconsin Department of Tourism
- Wisconsin Department of Transportation
- Wisconsin Film Festival
- Wisconsin Historical Society
- Wisconsin State Parks
- Wisconsin Welcome Centers
- Wisconsin's Major Airports
- Wisconsin's Year-Round Festivities
- WisDOT
- World's Largest Music Festival

Z

- Zoos and Wildlife Encounters

While perusing the "Wisconsin Travel Guide," you may easily find the information you need thanks to this thorough index. The index is your road map for accessing the amount of information in this trip book, whether you're looking for specific sites, activities, or useful suggestions.

Bonus: Travel Journal

Wisconsin Travel Journal

Date: _____   Transport: _____

Weather _____

SCHEDULE

Places:

Top Attractions

Notes

Wisconsin Travel Journal

Date: _____   Transport: _____

Weather

SCHEDULE	Places:

Top Attractions

Notes

Wisconsin Travel Journal

Date: _____   Transport: _____

| Weather |

SCHEDULE

Places:

Top Attractions

Notes

Wisconsin Travel Journal

Date: _____   Transport: _____

| Weather | ☁ | ☀ | 💧 | 🌙 | ❄ |

SCHEDULE

Places:

Top Attractions

Notes

Wisconsin Travel Journal

Date: _____ Transport: _____

| Weather |

SCHEDULE

Places:

Top Attractions

Notes

Wisconsin Travel Journal

Date: _____ Transport: _____

| Weather | ☁️ | ☀️ | 💧 | 🌙 | ❄️ |

SCHEDULE

Places:

Top Attractions

Notes

Wisconsin Travel Journal

Date: _____   Transport: _____

Weather

SCHEDULE

Places:

Top Attractions

Notes

Wisconsin Travel Journal

Date: _____   Transport: _____

Weather

SCHEDULE

Places:

Top Attractions

Notes

Wisconsin Travel Journal

Date: _____   Transport: _____

| Weather |

SCHEDULE

Places:

Top Attractions

Notes

Wisconsin Travel Journal

Date: _____   Transport: _____

| Weather |

SCHEDULE

Places:

Top Attractions

Notes

Printed in Great Britain
by Amazon

40807682R00059